Yard Down, Brayford

NORTH DEVON

North Devon is a rural landscape of small villages, rich pastures, secluded coves, and long, extensive, sandy beaches. The two ancient ports of Barnstaple and Bideford have grown up beside the wide estuary of the Taw and Torridge rivers.

Stretching southwards from these ports is the gentle pastoral countryside known as 'The Land of the Two Rivers', so vividly brought to life in the works of Henry Williamson. The warm equable climate, together with the nature of the countryside provides excellent recreational opportunities, particularly for the walker, fisherman and surfer, and remains a favourite destination for family beach holidays.

The Hartland Peninsula, on the western tip, is Devon's Land's End, and a landscape tempered by the punishing seas, and dramatic coastline. Often overlooked because of its isolation, a visit should be planned in with it's neighbour, Clovelly. The coast is in sharp contrast to the pastoral, inland country that runs in an Easterly direction from Great Torrington to Tiverton.

William Fricker

Low Tide, Appledore

APPLEDORE

One of North Devon's most attractive villages is set on the Torridge Estuary, with ancient inter-connecting streets, and rows of colour-washed cottages, reminiscent of the Greek Islands. It is worth exploring the little streets, and then to sit back by the harbor wall and watch the boats, come and go. Since the C14, it was a thriving fishing and trading village, and many of the fisherman's cottages date back to the Elizabethan period. Its centuries-old ship building tradition has had a precarious existence to this day.

The Quay, Instow

INSTOW

A popular holiday village with sandy beach, pedestrian ferry to Appledore that affords fine views of the Torridge Estuary. The home of the late, famous Test Match umpire, David Shepherd, who learnt his cricket at the North Devon CC. This ground overlooks the magnificent Torridge Estuary, and has a unique thatched Score Box and Pavilion. A worthy, stopping off point when riding the Tarka Trail.

Evening Light on Baggy

BAGGY POINT

Given to the National Trust in 1939 by Constance and Florence Hyde. A brazing circular 40-minute walk can be had up to the Point where you may be able to spy rock climbers traversing the wall, and fisherman waiting patiently for bass and conger to strike their lines. The spirit of this place inspired Henry Williamson to write many of his nature stories, so look out for the unusual plaque at the entrance.

The Dunes, Croyde Bay

CROYDE

This popular holiday, and all-year round surfing destination with its pretty thatched cottages, cafés, camp-sites, pubs and restaurants has become quite a fashionable resort on a par with Cornwall's Rock and Polzeath. The difference is in the rip curls and heavy waves that pound this shoreline. For they say "If you can surf Croyde, you can surf anywhere". The rips and currents are like no other. The Oyster Fall (just off Downend Point) sets the Bar.

The New & Old Bridge, Barnstaple

BARNSTAPLE

This is the principal town (and a former river-port) of North Devon, formerly known as Barum. It claims to be the oldest borough in the UK. Today, very much the route centre for the beaches of North Devon, and the new bridge crossing, from Sticklepath to Pottington has eased the bottleneck of traffic. It is also, a popular destination for cyclists' to refresh themselves beside the Tarka Trail. The C16 bridge, crook-spired church, Pannier Market, and Queen Anne's Walk provide a perspective of this town's rich historic past.

Evening Light on the Torridge

BIDEFORD

A lively and busy town on the Torridge Estuary, where to this day, cargo ships load and unload on the quay. In the C16 and C17, one of Britain's major seaports, handling cargoes from, and to, the New World. In the late C17, local merchants traded wool with Newfoundland sending out more ships than any other apart from London and Topsham. The fine 24-arch C15 bridge is one of the longest (677 ft) in the country, now overshadowed by the new bridge, down river.

BRAUNTON BURROWS & MARSH

Braunton Burrows. 2,400 acre National Nature Reserve, extending three miles along the estuary and coast. Abounds in wildlife; foxes, rabbits, hedgehogs, moles, weasels, mink, shrews, lizards and voles, also, butterflies, birds and rare plants. Free public access (except for an area sometimes closed for military training). Braunton Marsh. Former wild, tidal salt marsh now tamed into lush pasture land inhabited by cattle, wild flowers and bountiful birdlife. Protected by the Great Sea Bank built in 1808.

The Pealing Wreck, Crow Point

CROW POINT

This was naturally formed in 1809, and sticks out like a hook. It is 30 feet high in places, and topped with Marram grass. On the west side are, The Groynes, a collection of eroded wooden posts placed here to protect the sea wall. All sorts of debris washes up here from the maniacal tides; dead sheep, tyres and rough-hewn timbers. A great picnic spot.

The Waterfall & Lime Kiln

BUCK'S MILLS

The name derives from the Saxon "Bussac Hewise", meaning homestead. An isolated hamlet of romantic cottages lie at the bottom of a steep combe protected by high cliffs to either side, and from behind, thick woodland. In times gone by, the villagers made a living from fishing; herring, mackerel, lobster and prawn, as well as coastal lime burning needed for the fertilising of inland farms in order to neutralise the acid soil. The deep cut off the beach creates a swell popular with surfers.

The Harbour

CLOVELLY

A timeless village of cobbled streets, and quaint cottages, descend steeply to a harbor, and backdrop of rich blue sea. A former fishing port whose major wealth came from catching mackerel and herring. Today, a centre for small fishing trips, and visiting, day-trippers. When the fishing dried up, Clovelly men would seek employment digging the quarries on Lundy. Clovelly folk were a hardy breed. It was not just the men who worked their socks off, the women got stuck in, too. With the quarrying, and the making of fishing nets.

The Beach, Lobster & C14 Paintings

COMBE MARTIN

A long, straggling village bordered by some of the most beautiful countryside in England; a patchwork of rich, undulating, pastures that lead down to the small harbor, and beach. Nearby, Trentishoe Downs and the Heddon Valley, and beyond, the wild combes of Exmoor.

The Parish Church of St Peter Ad Vincula is a magnificent Perpendicular build with a fine C12 medieval Tower decorated with pinnacled battlements, and a superb collection of gargoyles. It stands at over 100 ft., and was built from the wealth of the silver industry. A typical Devon wagon roof, carved English rood screen, medieval windows, C14 paintings on the wainscotting and C15 font.

Bluebells, Foxgloves & Ancient Woodland, Braunton

COUNTRY LANES AND HEDGEROWS

The Cliffs & Beach at Low Tide

HARTLAND QUAY

A wild, and windswept corner of England, forever associated with smugglers of contraband, and a favourite landing spot for Sir Francis Drake and Sir Richard Grenville, Devon men. It's set on a treacherous coastline, and little wonder that the quay was swept away in 1841, 1887 and 1896. The present quay was rebuilt in 1979. The former Harbour Master's house is now the hotel. A wide road leads down to the slipway built for the transport of lime imported from South Wales.

View Over Heddon Valley & the River Heddon

HEDDON VALLEY

A beautiful, thickly wooded valley sided by steep hillsides, and arguably one of the most enchanting valleys in England. A path leads from behind the right side of the Inn down a tricky slope to the riverbank, and follows the river to Heddon Mouth, a rock-strewn beach with a massive old limekiln. The river is only fordable in dry months. The valley has numerous walks in all directions.

Aerial View & Verity

ILFRACOMBE

A popular holiday centre developed by the Victorians in the "Railway Age". A place of high cliffs, and rocky beaches, bordered behind by the sweeping Exmoor hills. Well situated for fine coastal walks, and trips to Exmoor and Lundy. The ancient harbour is a great attraction and has recently been refurbished, and is now home to Damien Hirst's controversial and much talked about sculpture, Verity.

The Beach

LEE BAY

Set in a sheltered combe known as Fuchsia Valley, for fuchsias grow wild in the hedgerows, and stone banks. The lane leads to Lee Bay, a beach of special marine biological interest that is overlooked by high cliffs, and the idyllic, Mill House. Low tide provides sand and rock pools, and steps to Sandy Cove, but beware of getting stranded from the inrushing tide, and note the special patterns of slate made by the swirling currents.

Watersmeet

LYNTON & LYNMOUTH

Twin villages in a spectacular setting; Lynton on its cliff edge, overhangs the small port of Lynmouth. The two are linked by a steep, wooded hill connected by footpaths, the steep road and a funicular railway powered by water tanks. The rivers, East and West Lyn, fall rapidly to the sea through picturesque wooded gorges. It is a popular walking centre and the steep, coastal road to Countisbury, and on to Minehead, is arguably one of the most scenic drives in England.

Cheviot Goats & Castle Rock

VALLEY OF ROCKS

A place of legend, and dramatic scenery, tempered by a micro-climate of swirling mists and brazen winds. The geologist will tell you it's a rock-strewn elevated valley created in the Ice Age; a mere collection of massive sandstone outcrops inhabited by Cheviot goats imported from Northumberland. A great place to scramble on the rocks, but the more refined walker will follow the coastal path and enjoy the spectacular views across the Bristol Channel towards South Wales.

Pink Magnolia & Hellebore

MARWOOD HILL GARDENS

An 18-acre garden blessed with many rare trees and shrubs. A rock and alpine garden, too, with lakes, a large bog garden, and a famous collection of camellias, considered the largest in the country. It also has a thriving Nursery with plant sales. Garden open daily dawn-dusk.

www.marwoodhillgarden.co.uk

The Morte Stone & Race

MORTE POINT

The scene of shipwrecks and loss of life, caused in no uncertain terms, by the notorious and treacherous currents of the Morte Race. In full flow, an amazing site, and an exhilarating spot on windy days. Look out for the razor-sharp rocks, sculptured by wind, rain and the sea. The Bull Point Lighthouse was built in 1879 to protect shipping from the dangers of Morte Point but is now an automatic station, a frail shadow of its former self.

The Beach

PEPPERCOMBE

An interesting section of the coast, often overlooked, but worthy of an inspection and detour to the beach for its geological interest; triassic marl colours in reds, browns and bright yellow, and the unusually coloured waterfall.
The castle was demolished by fierce storms, and eroding cliffs around 1900.

Avenue of Trees & Moss Bank

CHAPEL WOOD, SPREACOMBE

A circular walk takes you around this broadleaf woodland. Home to many species of birds including tawny owls, nuthatches, the great spotted and green woodpeckers, and all manner of wildlife; Red deer, brown hares and badgers, and rare dormice live here. The acidic soil allows for a limited splash of colour; bluebells, primroses and foxgloves. No dogs.

A Hazy Dawn & Rough Seas

SAUNTON SANDS

One of the truly great natural landscapes of Britain, for once seen, never forgotten. The extensive 4-mile stretch of compact sands is cleansed by the rolling Atlantic waves and overlooked by the giant rabbit warren, Braunton Burrows. Film location in WW11 for Vivien Leigh's Cleopatra, then used as a practice venue for the US Normandy Landings of June 1944. Surf popular with Long Boarders, and in the low tides it's possible to see rock forms that came down from Scotland in the Ice Age.

Shortboarder, Walking the Dog & Female Surfer, Saunton Sands

SURFING

Bird Sculpture near Yard & Trail Overlooking Putsborough Sands

TARKA TRAIL

An 180-mile trail (280km) follows the route taken by Tarka the Otter on his travels through "The Land of the Two Rivers", the Taw and Torridge, as depicted in Henry Williamson's classic novel Tarka the Otter written in the 1920s. The trail can be walked, but also offers on and off-road cycling. The trail becomes a dual-purpose walkway-cycleway allowing for relatively easy and safe cycling starting at Braunton. The route runs on tarmac beside the Taw Estuary to Barnstaple, via Instow, Great Torrington, all the way to Meeth.

Thatch Cottage, Umberleigh, River Taw & Harvested Meadow, Beam House, River Torridge

THE LAND OF THE TWO RIVERS

This was a term created by Henry Williamson who wrote many of his nature stories, and chronicles of Edwardian life, that were set within, and close to, the rivers Taw and Torridge. It is his story of *Tarka the Otter* that has been used to brand all manner of things within North Devon. One wonders if these marketing men have ever read Williamson's books? A good start would be his four-book chronicle of Edwardian life starting with *The Beautiful Years*, and ending with *The Pathway*.

Beach Huts & The Beach

WESTWARD HO!

Unusually, a seaside resort named after a book - it was established in 1863 in recognition of Charles Kingsley. Rudyard Kipling was educated at the United Services College, and some buildings survive as guest houses, and set Stalky & Co in the hills to south, now named 'Kipling Tors'. A quieter beach to surf becoming increasingly popular, away from the hordes of Croyde and Saunton. More recently, the town has seen an increase in new buildings, in marked contrast to the rows of colourful beach huts.

The Bay & Ancient Woodland

WOODY BAY

You will know of Woody Bay if you have walked the Coastal Footpath. Otherwise, this secretive cove may well remain hidden from you. To reach the cove you must walk down a steep zig-zag lane through ancient woodland. The Bay is overlooked by an artist's cottage, and the beach is strewn with pebbles and dangerous rocks. A waterfall pitches its worth onto the beach. You could be on a desert island until your reveille is woken by the tread of another walker.

Combesgate at Low Tide

WOOLACOMBE

From the headland above Morte Point the eye can see the great sweep of Woolacombe Bay. In the far distance, the jutting, flat plateau of Baggy Point and the sands of Putsborough, below. Behind, there are sand dunes and Chalacombe Hill, and thankfully, little else. For this landscape is protected from development by the National Trust. Woolacombe is one of the finest beach resorts in the UK, and the world. The two-mile long sandy beach has witnessed many happy family holidays, and decades of rip curls, peaks and troughs, and clean waves loved by generations of surfers.

View from Woolacombe Down

PUTSBOROUGH

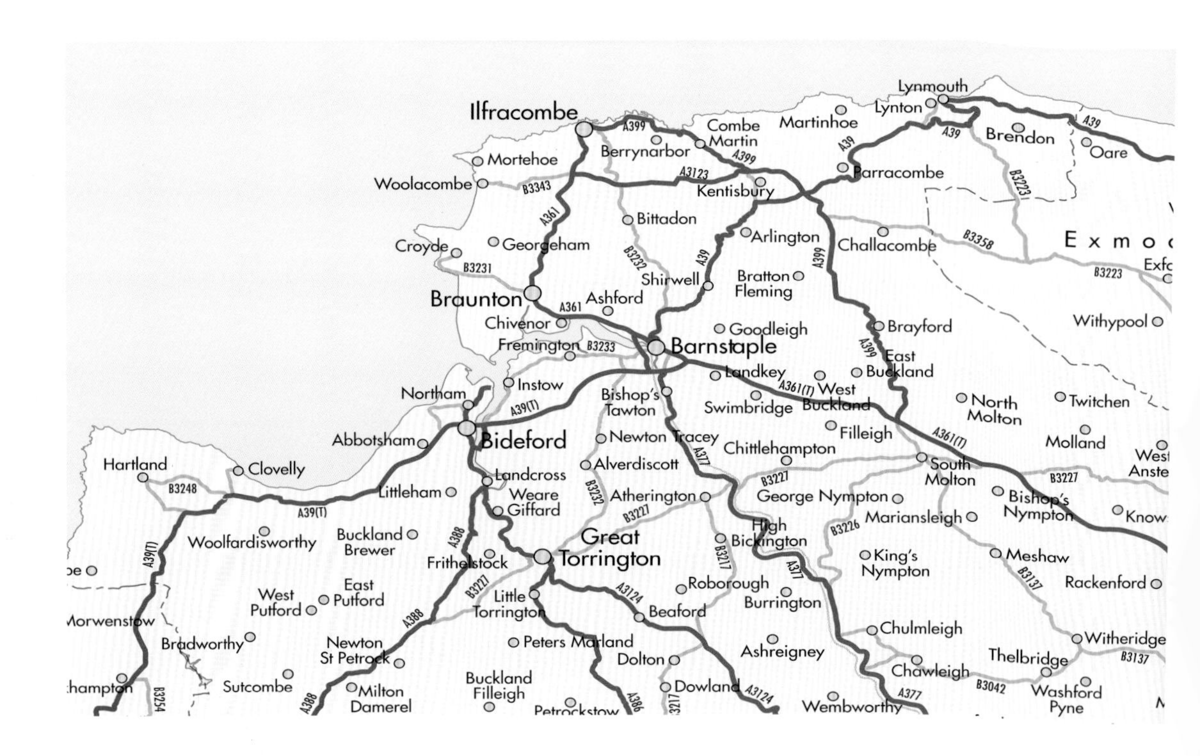

Text: William Fricker © William Fricker
Photography: William Fricker © William Fricker
First Published in the United Kingdom, in 2013,
by Goldeneye, Braunton, Devon EX33 1HW
In Association with

www.williamfrickerphotography.com

Design & Layout: Harry Fricker - www.harryfricker.com

Back Cover image of lobsters photographed at Mortehoe Shellfish.

A CIP catalogue record for this book is available from the British Library.

ISBN 9 781859652 19 0

 Printed in England